AN UNAUTHORIZED ROCKOGRAPHY

THE ROLLING STONES

The Greatest Rock Band

Heather Miller

REBELS OF ROCK

Enslow Publishers, Inc.
40 Industrial Road
Box 398
Berkeley Heights, NJ 07922
USA
http://www.enslow.com

Library of Congress Cataloging-in-Publication Data

Miller, Heather.

   The Rolling Stones : the greatest rock band / Heather Miller.

      p. cm. — (Rebels of rock)

   Includes bibliographical references and index.

   Summary: "A biography of British rock band the Rolling Stones"—Provided by publisher.

   ISBN 978-0-7660-3231-6

   1. Rolling Stones—Juvenile literature. 2. Rock musicians—Biography—Juvenile literature.

I. Title.

   ML3930.R64M55 2010

   782.42166092'2—dc22

   [B]   2009012296

ISBN-13: 978-1-59845-209-9 (paperback ed.)

Printed in the United States of America

052010 Lake Book Manufacturing, Inc., Melrose Park, IL

10 9 8 7 6 5 4 3 2 1

To Our Readers: This book has not been authorized by the Rolling Stones or its successors.

We have done our best to make sure all Internet Addresses in this book were active and appropriate when we went to press. However, the author and the publisher have no control over and assume no liability for the material available on those Internet sites or on other Web sites they may link to. Any comments or suggestions can be sent by e-mail to comments@enslow.com or to the address on the back cover.Every effort has been made to locate all copyright holders of material used in this book. If any errors or omissions have occurred, corrections will be made in future editions of this book.

♻ Enslow Publishers, Inc., is committed to printing our books on recycled paper. The paper in every book contains 10% to 30% post-consumer waste (PCW). The cover board on the outside of each book contains 100% PCW. Our goal is to do our part to help young people and the environment too!

Illustration Credits: Associated Press, pp. 4, 8, 76; Norm Betts/Rex USA/Courtesy Everett Collection, p. 80; © Buena Vista Pictures/Courtesy Everett Collection, p. 85; Andre Csillag/Rex Features/Courtesy Everett Collection, p. 74; Everett Collection, p. 62; Dezo Hoffmann/Rex Features/Courtesy Everett Collection, pp. 32, 59, 64; L.J. van Houten/Rex USA/Courtesy Everett Collection, p. 35; Hulton Archive/Getty Images, p. 50; Michael Ochs Archives/Getty Images, p. 71; © Paramount Classics/Courtesy Everett Collection, p. 90; © Pictorial Press Ltd/Alamy, pp. 29, 40; Terry O'Neill/Rex USA/Courtesy Everett Collection, p. 25; Peter Sanders/Rex Features/Courtesy Everett Collection, p. 20; © Topham/The Image Works, pp. 15, 53.

Cover Illustration: Associated Press

CONTENTS

In September 1965, the Rolling Stones performed at Waldbühne in Germany.

FRENZIED FANS

One mid-September morning in 1965, Berlin newspapers described the aftermath of a destructive night: forty-four smashed automobiles, fifteen cars of the elevated train damaged, twenty thousand stadium seats upturned and destroyed, and seventy-seven people injured—with twenty-eight of those sent to the hospital. Three hundred people were arrested as four hundred police officers tried to reclaim order. Had the German city been attacked by a foreign military? Were the citizens revolting against an oppressive government? Surprisingly, the answer to both questions is no. The damages to the city were inflicted by Germans driven to a frenzy by something much more common and seemingly innocent. It was music that produced this wild energy. More specifically it was rock-and-roll music, played by one of the greatest groups of musicians our world has ever seen—the Rolling Stones.[1]

The Rolling Stones stepped out of the airplane and onto German soil in front of over one thousand screaming fans. It was the second week of September 1965, when the band arrived in Berlin, Germany. Berlin was one of the band's first stops scheduled during their German tour. Members Mick Jagger, Brian Jones, Keith Richards, Charlie Watts, and Bill Wyman were full of energy and ready to play. Their arrival was hurried as military agents from the four countries that shared control of Berlin at the time ushered the band to their vehicles. Even twenty years after World War II, the undercurrents of war ran strong through Berlin. As a result, security measures were not taken lightly. Military leaders from Great Britain, France, Russia, and the United States took control of the Rolling Stones' arrival, allowing the band to enter the city without incident.[2]

The Berlin concert was held at the Waldbühne, which was also the place where Adolf Hitler, the dictator of Germany responsible for killing millions of innocent people during World War II, made speeches to his aggressive followers. On the night of the concert, the band prepared for the show in dressing rooms that were once used as military bunkers. With police and security dogs at the ready, it was time for the show to begin. Jagger, Jones, Richards, Watts, and Wyman trudged through the woods, then navigated through a series of underground storehouses in order to reach the stage. After an interesting walk to the stadium, the band stood before a crowd of over twenty thousand fans.[3] The intense energy felt at the event couldn't be denied.

Finally, the Rolling Stones began to play. After just one song, the energy of the crowd became dangerous and many fans began to riot. The Rolling Stones were ordered to stop playing and take a break. Security officials and police officers spent twenty minutes regaining order before the band could return to finish their twenty-five-minute set.[4] After the concert, police used rubber clubs called truncheons, to force the huge and frenzied crowd out of the stadium.[5]

The band was quickly whisked away to the Gehrhaus Hotel inside armored military vehicles. Oblivious to the chaos they left behind, the band settled in for food, drink, and relaxation. But it wasn't long before they began to hear sounds of the riot, which had quickly escalated, coming from several miles away. Even though they knew things had been out of control during the concert, Jagger and the rest of the band had no idea how destructive the fans had become until they read the headlines in the next morning's newspaper. Jagger said of the evening, "There were wild scenes, but we missed most of it. A lot of it—such as the breaking up of seats—

occurred after we'd gone. It was like a football [soccer] crowd gone mad. I was a bit scared." [6]

Marianne Koch, a reporter who attended the concert, described the events as being quite horrific. "Now I know what hell is like. My job has taught me to be brave, but in the Waldbühne I learned what fear is like. It is a mob out of

SECURITY GUARDS HOLD BACK SCREAMING FANS IN 1965 IN GERMANY.

control, stampeding at the entrances. I was almost crushed. The air was filled with the yelling of the crowd and the hammering beat of the band. It was like a witch's cauldron and the whole place glowed with the atmosphere."[7]

Once all was quiet, city officials began to analyze why and how such chaos had erupted. Most officials agreed that the crowd had simply been too large. At that time in history, rock-and-roll concerts were very new and security plans to keep both band members and fans safe had not yet been developed. The Waldbühne was not intended to hold a crowd of that size. Furthermore, the community was certainly not prepared for tens of thousands of teenagers pumped up on adrenaline and alcohol. The Rolling Stones did not encourage violence, nor did they prompt fans to act destructively. It was the energy of rock and roll that seemed to put the teenagers over the edge. The concert brought forth an explosion of energy that is typical of many teenagers. Because the reaction to rock-and-roll music was so extreme and new, things simply tumbled out of control. Soon after the Rolling Stones concert, the Berlin Senate banned all large concerts and limited rock-and-roll crowds to only a few hundred fans.

More Violent Reaction

The incident in Berlin was not unique or isolated. Unfortunately, disruption and destruction seemed to follow the Rolling Stones to many other cities they toured during that summer.

In Hamburg, Germany, wild fans were sprayed with water cannons to break up a street fight that took seven hundred policemen over six hours to control. While in Essen, Germany, at the Grugahalle Stadium, the Stones were forced to play behind a series of steel crash barriers set up to protect them.

A nameless policeman from Essen told the *Daily Mail*, "I have seen nothing like this since the old days of a Nazi or Communist rally."[8] When the Stones traveled to Italy, a bomb threat in Vienna caused a delay but ultimately nothing was found.

Not surprisingly, some cities canceled shows when they heard of the chaotic destruction that the Rolling Stones stimulated. Cities that did hold shows sent the band hefty bills to cover the losses sustained by their communities. Berlin charged the band 271,571.50 deutsche marks ($178,675) for stadium damage.[9] The city officially classified the Rolling Stones' sound as "noise" and not music. After forcing the band to cancel, the Opera Theater held the band responsible for 23,000 deutsche marks ($15,130) to cover the losses incurred due to the termination of the show. However, even after paying fines and taxes, the Rolling Stones considered the summer a huge success.[10]

Press coverage was heavy as reporters followed the band from city to city, waiting to see what sort of drama would follow them. Fans became more excited by the element of danger that the band inadvertently carried with them. A rebellious band was certainly appealing to rebellious teens. The Rolling Stones were exactly what thousands of fans had been waiting for. In return, fans were exactly what the band needed. With a flurry of fans and a reputation for rebellion, nothing could stop the momentum of the Rolling Stones.

THE LIVES OF LEGENDS

The Rolling Stones are a band made up of members who lived as rebels. They were all raised in rough, English neighborhoods during a time of war. The members of the Rolling Stones grew up during difficult times. Some members experienced abuse and neglect. They found each other as teens and they began to play rock and roll. As young men, they did not allow themselves to be led by rules and authority. Instead, the members of the Rolling Stones followed their passions and thrived on spontaneity. Their intense energy attracted a generation of young fans from all over the world. Talent, creativity, and excitement made the Rolling Stones the rock-and-roll band with the longest sustained success story of any band that has ever played.

Mick Jagger

On December 7, 1940, a young man and woman stood before the altar in a small church in Dartford, Kent, England, to join together in marriage. The bride's name was Eva Scuttse and her fiancé was Joe Jagger. That winter was a difficult time to be married. It followed an autumn in which bombs fell on their city for sixty-nine nights throughout October, November, and December. Eva and Joe's wedding was held during the peak of World War II in a church darkened by black curtains. Curtains blocked the light during blackouts, a time when the town experienced mandatory lights-out in order to become invisible to the enemy bombers that flew above the city. During the first two years of the Jagger marriage, eleven thousand in Dartford County were bombed and over one hundred fifty citizens were killed. Times were definitely difficult, but even so, the Jaggers wanted to start a family.

On July 26, 1943, Joe and Eva Jagger welcomed a son into their family, Michael Philip Jagger. Although the war was still raging, many people began to feel there was an end in sight. With the birth of their new son, the Jaggers were more hopeful than ever that the war would soon end. One month after Michael was born, fourteen people were killed and eleven were injured when a bomb was dropped less than one mile away from the Jagger home.

The Jaggers struggled with daily life during wartime. The amount of food people were allowed to consume was rationed, or limited. Eggs were scarce. Each adult in a household was given only two eggs each week. Sugar was limited to two pounds per month and only three ounces of bacon could be purchased for each person each week. The winter after Michael (nicknamed Mike) was born, coal, the main source of household heat, was also rationed. The family experienced many cold winter nights. Time after time, the Jaggers took cover under their staircase as bombs fell throughout their neighborhood.

World War II ended just five months before Mike turned two years old. Although he experienced war as a very young child, Mike was emotionally affected by the uncertainty of war. His earliest childhood memory is that of his mother removing the darkening cloths that covered the windows of their home during blackouts. As the cloths were removed, a symbolic rebirth was experienced through the entire community as people began to thrive again, excited to live life to its fullest.

Even as a child, little Mike Jagger lived life with full force. His mother recalled one particular phase Mike went through as a preschooler: "When he was four he had a phase of hitting people for no reason. Once, on holiday, we were walking along

Mick Jagger in 1967

a beach when Mike knocked down every single sandcastle we came across. Even ones that little boys were still building."[1]

During the fall of 1947, Mike began his academic career at Maypole Primary School, where his teachers did not always appreciate his high energy and active personality. Just before Christmas that same year, Mike's brother, Christopher, was born.

A few years passed and Mike moved on to Wentworth Primary School where he was known as a particularly intelligent, yet still very active, child. Mike was popular with other students but not a favorite student of his teachers. His lifelong goals were well established at an early age as he announced that one day he would be rich and own a very expensive, flashy car—specifically a Cadillac.

It was at Wentworth County School where Mike met bandmate Keith Richards. The two were friends, but not best buddies. Jagger told *Rolling Stone* magazine about his lifelong friendship with Keith. "I can't remember when I didn't know him," said Jagger. "We lived one street away; his mother knew my mother, and we were at primary school together from [ages] 7 to 11. We used to play together, and we weren't the closest friends, but we were friends."[2] When the boys turned eleven years old, they went to different schools and eventually lost track of each other for several years.

Jagger spent his teen years developing as an academic. He passed the Eleven Plus exam (an aptitude test used to

determine school placement) with strong scores, which led to his admittance to Dartford Grammar School. He dove head-first into his studies and turned away from friendships. Jagger recalls his early adolescence as being a bit on the boring side. "I never got to have a raving adolescence between the age of 12 and 15, because I was concentrating on my studies . . . but that's what I wanted to do and I enjoyed it."[3]

In the early 1950s, when rock and roll started to grab the attention of English teens, the whole scene surprisingly bored Mike. One might think that a rock-and-roll legend would have been instantly mesmerized by the energy and sounds of the new music genre that seemed to be casting a spell across the entire world. That was not the case with Jagger, who described most of the musicians as being "waffly pop" sing-ers.[4] He was, however, obsessed with the sound of blues, a type of music that originated on American slave plantations. The music was filled with soul and emotion, and to Jagger it was "real music."[5] Blues was the music that captured Mike's attention and his soul.

Little Richard was one of the first artists who made Mike stand up and take notice. One song in particular, "Good Golly Miss Molly," was Mike's favorite. Mike once asked his father for some money so he could pick up the track at a record shop. Mike was left with empty pockets and an empty record player. Like most parents at the time, the Jaggers did not like rock-and-roll music and preferred their children to simply ignore the whole scene.

Mike's parents did not encourage him to pursue music, nor did his family see any particular musical talent in their son. Mike's brother, Christopher, once said, "Mike had no interest in music. . . . He didn't take piano lessons or anything like that. I think his main ambition as a boy was to be rich."[6]

During the summer of 1955, twelve-year-old Mike worked on an American military base as a coach's helper for a summer youth program. During that impressionable summer, Mike grew even more motivated to become rich. He knew that someday, somehow, he would figure out a way to become both famous and wealthy. With visions of mansions and a Cadillac drifting through his daydreams, Mike went back to school in the fall with a new set of plans. He stayed with his studies and continued to be very successful in school—but the whole time, he kept one eye focused on money and America.

Mike also began to focus on music. He discovered more artists who played the style of music that he loved. Muddy Waters, a legendary blues artist, was one of Mike's favorite musicians, as was Big Bill Broonzy. Mike began collecting records and becoming more and more connected with the sound. Mike put a great deal of energy behind his new obsession with music. Just like everything he did, Mike jumped in headfirst and started looking for a group of guys to jam with. It wasn't long before all the pieces came together. Eventually,

Jagger reunited with his childhood friend Keith Richards, and was happy to discover that Richards had also been hypnotized by music. It was a trance neither man would ever break free from.

Keith Richards

Unlike Jagger, Keith Richards knew he was a musician at an early age. Keith grew up in a musical family. His mother, Doris, introduced him to jazz, a type of music involving complicated rhythms first played by African Americans. She also encouraged Keith to sing, and signed him up for the school choir. Keith excelled at singing. He was considered a soprano, who sang the highest pitches within the melody. Keith also had perfect pitch, meaning he hit each note exactly right, without singing off key. He stood out in his choir as the strongest singer. Keith and two other singers from Dartford were chosen from hundreds of other youngsters to sing in Westminster Abbey, a famous church in London. On Tuesday, June 2, 1953, Keith experienced his first taste of fame when he sang before the Queen of England. His performance was breathtaking. Winston Churchill, the British prime minister at the time, was "moved to tears" by the sound of Keith's voice. Little did the world know that twenty years later the little boy in the choir would move on to become a famous rock musician.[7]

Keith
Richards
in 1969

Doris Richards knew her son was not into typical "boy" activities. She knew his interest in music would take over and said, "Keith always sang to the radio or a record and he knew all the words. He tried the Boy Scouts, but that didn't last. Nor did he enjoy school, neither the work, nor the sport."[8]

Though his mother's support certainly helped Keith as a young musician, he was most influenced by his grandfather, Gus Dupree. Dupree played in a dance band during the 1930s. Keith remembers his grandfather having an upright piano in his home. But Keith wasn't interested in the piano. The Spanish guitar that could always be found resting on top of his grandfather's piano fascinated him more. One day his grandfather said, "Well, now you can reach it, you can take it down."[9] Richards remembered playing the guitar for the first time and said, "It's uncanny, as if he had his eye on me as a guitar player before I knew it."[10] Many years after his grandfather died, Richards's family told him that the guitar was placed on the piano only when Dupree knew his grandson was coming to visit.

Keith may have found his life's passion at a younger age than his friend Mike Jagger, but his family's experience was a bit more challenging than young Mike's. Doris and Bert Richards were married on December 17, 1938. Five years after the wedding, the Richards family found themselves raising a baby in a war zone.

Keith was born on December 18, 1943, right in the middle of the Second World War. His father, who worked for the electric company, was soon drafted into the army.[11] When Keith was only a year old, he and his mother were forced to evacuate their home in Dartford. Their house was located directly in the path of an aggressive bombing campaign led by Nazi Germany. Bert suffered a severe leg injury while fighting in the war. He was transported to a hospital in Mansfield, Nottinghamshire in England. Keith and his mother moved near the hospital and remained there for the rest of the war.

The sirens and explosions of the war frightened Keith so much so that to this day, he still reacts when sounds remind him of those violent days. "If I'm walking through a hotel and I hear a TV, and it's playing one of those Blitz movies the hair goes up on the back of my head and I get goosebumps. It's a reaction . . . something I picked up from what happened in the first eighteen months of my life," said Richards.[12]

Wartime spilled into Keith's early school days. Just like for Mike, food rations were a part of life for Keith. At school he and his classmates were given a medicine bottle full of orange juice at the beginning of each month. Richards explained, "That was your vitamin C for the month!"[13]

Keith attended school during the 1950s at Wentworth Primary School, which is where he met Mike for the first time. As one story explains, Keith's first encounter with Mike was made when the boys were seven years old. Keith remembers talking with friends on the back porch of their school when a young boy carrying a chemistry set approached. The boy with the chemistry set was Mike. Mike turned to Keith and declared, "When I grow up, I'm going to blow things up. I'm gonna blow up the whole world!"[14] After making his unusual statement, Mike dashed away down the hall. He made quite an impression on Keith. Keith soon realized that the boy with the chemistry set lived close to his home. They became friends and played together for several years, until the Richards family moved to the other side of town. After the move the boys lost track of each other, but the separation was only temporary.

As a student, Keith was in no way like Mike. While Mike worked hard for good grades and self-improvement, Keith was considered a slacker. Mike passed the Eleven Plus exam with high scores. Keith failed it miserably and was placed in technical school.[15] Even though Keith was placed on a track in school that was designed to be less academically challenging, he still found school to be difficult. He failed his third year in technical school and was forced to repeat his studies. Soon after that, he was expelled from school altogether. Luckily, the school headmaster saw a glimmer of talent in the seemingly unmotivated student and enrolled Keith in the Sidcup Art College.[16]

As a young adult attending Sidcup, Richards met a fellow student named Dick Taylor. Richards said, "Dick Taylor was the first guy I played with. We played together on acoustic guitars. Then I got an amplifier like a little beat-up radio.

We formed a country western band. The first time I got onstage was a sports dance at Eltham, near Sidcup."[17] As a young child, Keith often announced he would one day be a guitar-playing cowboy. That debut gig with his own little country band was Keith's first glimpse of his dream beginning to come true.

Brian Jones

There were other boys growing up in England with dreams of playing in rock-and-roll bands. One of those boys was named Brian Jones. Brian was born on February 28, 1942, in Cheltenham, England.[18] Brian was not welcomed by a loving family. A premature baby, he suffered from fetal alcohol syndrome, a result of his mother's drinking habit during pregnancy. Because of his condition, Brian's growth may have been slowed, causing him to reach adulthood as a particularly small and frail man. Brian was challenged by a long list of illnesses, many of them mental disorders. He was afflicted with attention deficit disorder, hyperactivity, clinical depression, and bipolar disorder. He was also challenged by asthma, a breathing disorder; arthritis, a disease that causes severe joint pain; narcolepsy, a sleeping disorder; and fibromyalgia, a disease that causes severe pain throughout the body.[19]

To make things worse, Brian was born into an abusive family. His mother and father both subjected him to physical and mental abuse. His mother, Louisa Jones, would grab

Brian Jones
in 1964

fistfuls of her son's hair with such brutal force that Brian felt sure she would rip it out of his scalp. His father, Lewis Jones, constantly threw insults at Brian, shouting things like, "Stand straight, for heaven's sake! Can't you do anything right, Brian?" After causing his son to fall down a flight of stairs, Mr. Jones shouted at his son, "Stop acting like a girl! You're a little crybaby, just like your mum! Be a man, for heaven's sake!"[20] In many European families at the time, the firstborn son was regarded as a precious gift and a source of pride and joy. For Brian, this was not the case. He was thought of as a burden, an unwanted child, disconnected from his parents in almost every way.

Despite all of his hardships, Brian was gifted with an extremely high level of intelligence. He graduated from elementary school with grades high enough to grant his acceptance into the elite Cheltenham Grammar School for Boys. There he excelled in English, creative writing, chemistry, math, and music. Because schoolwork was easy for him, Brian was often bored with his studies. Teachers described him as an intelligent rebel who only applied himself to his studies when the mood struck him.[21]

Brian had a rebellious edge that was attractive to friends. He once said, "My friends stuck by me because my mind was entertaining and amusing, and they always wondered what I was going to do next. I'd send them off into outer space with thoughts of all kinds of fun things, like putting a frog up a teacher's dress. I wasn't a fancy dance man, but I knew I could captivate my audience with my mind and I always kept them entertained, happy, and amused. I was the king of the nerds!"[22]

The attention Brian received from his adoring friends filled a great hole that was left by his distant parents. Brian discovered the magic of entertaining others and the love his audience gave him.

As Brian began to experiment with music, he discovered that his soul could find refuge from his pain in the music that he played and listened to. Brian's mother did play a small role in fostering his musical talent. She began teaching him how to play the piano when he was just six years old. He quickly grew past his mother's skill level and moved on to a more advanced piano teacher who also found it difficult to challenge Brian as he progressed at an incredibly rapid pace. Brian also played the clarinet, guitar, and alto saxophone. By age ten, he was writing his own music.

Like the other members of the Rolling Stones, Brian was particularly drawn to the sound of blues music. He felt a strong connection to the style that came from the sorrow of slaves forced to work in North America prior to the American Civil War. Most people would agree that young Jones must have felt a personal connection to the expressions of suffering sung by slaves. Brian hoped to invent his own style of music that would one day capture listeners in a similar way.

As a young teen, music played a particularly important role in Brian's life. Time after time, Brian was kicked out of his own home for breaking various household rules. He was forced to search through garbage cans for food scraps and to sleep in abandoned buildings. During those lonely nights, Brian created music in his mind, tapping out rhythms on empty cans while trying to escape the incredible pain he was experiencing. Jones believed that during his time living on the street he learned valuable lessons about the human spirit. He felt strongly that music could help a person escape from any type of pain or suffering and he made it his goal to create music that would help people do so.[23] He later did, as the creator of the Rolling Stones.

Bill Wyman

Born on October 24, 1936, in London, England, Bill Wyman was the oldest member of the Rolling Stones. Like the other band members, Bill had a war-scarred childhood. Bill's family was challenged with a heavy load of hardship. He grew up in the depths of poverty. His mother heated water on the stove each week for bath day. A metal tub was set up in the kitchen and each family member took turns washing up, never dumping the water until the last family member had finished. The lineup for bath time began with the youngest child. Bill, being the oldest, ended up with the last bath, which was taken in dirty water. "I naturally ended up in filthy water, emerging

Bill
Wyman
in 1965

almost dirtier than when I got in, attempting to dry off with a wet, five-times-used towel that hung on the back of the door."[24] The family also shared one toothbrush and because toothpaste was rather expensive, they scrubbed their teeth with salt.

Besides growing up poor, the Wymans were surrounded by crime and violence. Their neighborhood was less than ideal for raising a family. Bill's parents, William and Molly, stressed honesty and integrity and tried to raise their children with these qualities. "We weren't a particularly religious family," said Wyman, "but we were expected to do the right thing."[25]

Bill took his schoolwork seriously. He scored well on his Eleven Plus exam and was one of three boys from a class of fifty-two students to be accepted to the Beckenham and Penge Grammar School for Boys. There he took piano lessons and also played the clarinet. Bill had a difficult time fitting in at school. Most of the other students came from middle-class families whereas Bill was nowhere near middle class. His classmates criticized him for his working-class accent and claimed he spoke like a low-class citizen. As Bill learned proper English at school, he began to speak differently at home. This brought on teasing from his family members and neighborhood friends. Wyman described his difficult situation when he said, "If I went to school and spoke normally, they would poke fun at my working-class accent, but if I tried 'talking posh' as they called it when I got home, I was mocked by

everyone around me."[26] Unfortunately, Bill had to leave school before he graduated. His father insisted he get a job to help raise money to support the family.[27] He walked away from school in March 1953, just two months before graduating. Bill was very upset by his father's decision, but there was nothing he could do.[28]

For the next several years, Wyman held several different jobs. He worked as a bookkeeper and then served in the military. When his military service was over, Wyman worked for a company that imported meat. After that he earned a paycheck as a storekeeper. He found love and was married in 1959.

In 1960, Wyman gathered a group of friends and started a band called the Cliftons. He played a bass guitar that he made himself and through much practice he became a solid musician. It wouldn't be long before Wyman would stumble across an opportunity that would change his life forever.

Charlie Watts

Born on June 2, 1941, in London, Charlie Watts grew up in a small, plain house and had a rather ordinary childhood. As an adult, Charlie Watts was nowhere near ordinary. In 1964, he was named the second most famous drummer in the world— second only to Ringo Starr, the drummer for the Beatles who just happened to be the world's most popular rock-and-roll band.

In 1948, the Watts family moved from London to start a

Charlie Watts in the mid-1960s

new life in Kingsbury, England. In Kingsbury, Charlie was surrounded by parks, farmland, and many playgrounds. Charlie was an athletic child. He particularly enjoyed running sprints, soccer (called football in England), and bowling. Lillian Watts, Charlie's mother, once said, "He was a big boy with strong legs. We often thought he would become a footballer [soccer player]."[29] But Charlie also had a short temper and frequently found himself in trouble after starting fistfights on the playground. Because he was a rather violent child, he was not encouraged by coaches to join any teams.

Charlie did not show signs of his musical interests until he turned eleven years old. He did not take any musical lessons as some of the other members of the Rolling Stones did. He did not even come from a musical family. Watts once described the musical talents of his family saying, "I reckon the only instrument any of them could play at home was the gramophone or record player."[30]

The 1952 release of the single "Flamingo" by saxophonist Earl Bostic unleashed a new passion for Charlie. The song was the first that really connected with the eleven-year-old and it opened up the world of jazz music. Charlie began to seek out jazz recordings. He studied the lives of the musicians he loved. Duke Ellington and Count Basie were two of Charlie's favorite jazz composers while Benny Goodman and Woody Herman captured his ear with their fast-paced swing.[31] The sounds Charlie loved most came from an era he had missed: the swing era of the 1920s and '30s. "I'd like to have gone to the Savoy Ballroom [to see] Chick Webb, I think," said Watts. "I'd love to have seen Ellington at the Cotton Club and have dressed for the occasion. I'd love to have seen Louis Armstrong, probably at the Roseland Ballroom in Chicago in the 1930s with a big band behind him."[32] Charlie listened to records over and over again. As he listened he absorbed the rhythm and beat, making both a part of his soul.

Charlie began to experiment with making music on his own. He picked up a secondhand banjo and tried to learn how to play, but he quickly became frustrated with it. "I took the thing apart, made a stand for it out of wood and played on the round skin part with brushes," said Watts.[33] Finally, Charlie had connected with a drum! Charlie's parents bought him a drum kit for Christmas. He taught himself to play while listening to his collection of jazz records. The rest is rock-and-roll history.

Ronnie Wood

"My brothers and I were the first in my family to be born on dry land," Ronnie Wood explains in his autobiography.[34] The newest member of the Rolling Stones came from a family with an unusual history. Ronnie's parents, known to friends as Archie and Lizzie, lived on a barge they called the *Orient.* They were often referred to as "water gypsies." When they decided to have children, the boat was given up and they

Ronnie Wood in 1982

moved into a small home. Ronnie was born on June 1, 1947, in Yiewsley, England. He was the third of three boys. Ronnie was definitely not a calm child. "I was a hyperactive child and Mum worried that I'd run out the kitchen door and roll down the back steps, so she tethered me to the leg of the kitchen table," Wood later said of himself.[35]

Ronnie attended St. Martin's Church of England Secondary School, just blocks away from his home. As a boy, he was very small. Because he was so light, Wood claims he rode to school in an unusual way. The family dog, Chum, was a large sheepdog, large enough to carry Ronnie on his back all the way to school. According to Wood, every day at 3:15 P.M., Chum would walk back to school to meet him at the end of his day.[36]

Ronnie was an average student who earned mostly Bs on his report card. His lowest grades, Cs, were earned in religious education, mathematics, and music theory. Ronnie excelled in art and earned an A in that class. His teacher complimented his achievements by stating he should consider focusing on art in secondary school.[37]

As a teenager, Ronnie focused on art. He consumed every piece of paper in the house and had to wait for his father to bring more scraps home from work. "I especially loved to draw horses and was inspired by the early editions of [a magazine called] *Buffalo Bill*," said Wood.[38]

Ronnie longed to earn a living as an artist, but his talent

did not produce a paycheck. To earn money as a teenager Ronnie took a job as a potato picker, which didn't last long. He couldn't stand working early hours in freezing cold weather. After potato picking he worked as a butcher's assistant delivering meat by bicycle. After several jobs that were completely unrelated to the arts, Ronnie found work with a real estate agency where he painted "For Sale" signs, his first job as a paid artist.[39]

While art was his first love, music also began to take hold of Ronnie. His first introduction to music was at home. His father used to invite old friends from the river gypsy crowd to the Wood family home nearly every weekend. Many of their friends, and everyone in the Wood family, played an instrument of some kind. Weekends with the Woods were filled with crazy parties and music.

As a boy, Ronnie watched his family play and wanted to experience the joy that they shared while performing. He first learned to play the washboard, a primitive percussion instrument played by rubbing a stick across a sheet of corrugated metal. Ronnie learned to play well enough to join his brother Ted at a gig at the Marlborough Cinema in Yiewsley High Street when Ronnie was nine years old.[40]

Ronnie's interest in music grew. He wanted to play the guitar but he didn't have the money to buy one of his own. He was lucky enough to get his hands on one for a few weeks when a friend gave him a guitar to play. Ronnie assumed the guitar was a gift. When he learned that he had to return it he was heartbroken. He practiced hard, and carried fret charts in his pocket that told where to put his fingers to play chords on the guitar. For Ronnie, giving the guitar back was like giving away a part of himself. His friends knew how much the instrument meant to him, so they pooled their money and bought him his own acoustic guitar. Wood said, "It was a lovely acoustic . . . it hurt my fingers to play it. My hands were ready to deal with the blisters and cramps and I wasn't going to let the pain stop me."[41] Lucky for the rest of us, Ronnie didn't let a few blisters slow him down.

Together

The members of the Rolling Stones were bonded by a childhood affected by the violence and fear of World War II. Their love of blues and jazz music brought them all together and their amazing talent brought them to the rest of the world.

BOYS WITH THE BLUES

The Gathering of Stones

On what seemed to be a perfectly ordinary day in October 1960, Mike Jagger walked to the local train station carrying a stack of American rhythm and blues records under his arm. Knowing they were prized possessions, and a rare find in England, Jagger held the stack carefully. With the music he loved filling his arms, Jagger seemed to be traveling down a path of good fortune when he bumped into a long lost friend. Keith Richards happened to be taking the train on the same day. Richards, who had also been smitten with the sound of blues music, was excited to see his old friend.

THE ROLLING STONES IN 1964

Jagger shared his records with Richards. The two of them reconnected quickly.

Jagger said, "We started to go to each other's house and play these records. And then we started to go to other people's houses to play other records. You know, it's the time in your life when you're almost stamp collecting this stuff."[1]

Jagger and Richards soon learned of each other's interests in forming a band. Jagger explained, "I can't quite remember how all this worked. Keith always played the guitar, from even when he was five. And he was keen on country music, cowboys. But obviously at some point, Keith, he had his guitar with this electric-guitar pickup. And he played it for me. So I said, 'Well, I sing, you know? And you play the guitar.' Very obvious stuff."[2]

While Jagger may make the band sound like it just fell together effortlessly, the real story is a bit more complicated. Just as all rock-and-roll bands seem to work through a great deal of drama before they make it to the top, the Rolling Stones were no different. They had to work through their fair share of hard times and struggle.

No Instant Success

The first time Richards took the stage was in the middle of winter, 1960. He played at a scout hall with two of his friends. They called themselves the Sidcup Shaggers and they struggled through about six Johnny Cash, Hank Snow, and Elvis Presley songs. The concert announcer was wasting his words when he reminded the audience to leave quietly as most of the small group that had gathered to watch the show had left long before the band had finished playing. Richards remembers the rest of the evening as being just as awful as he "spent the night freezing in a bus shelter. . . . That was my introduction to show business," he said.[3]

Richards may not have had much luck with his first gig, but his love for music did not fade. Richards and Jagger hooked up with another friend, Dick Taylor, who played bass guitar. Richards had met Taylor at Sidcup Art College, the school they both attended.

They rotated between each other's homes on weekends, practicing until their parents made them stop. Neither the Jagger household nor the Richards household could continue to tolerate the band's practicing. Luckily, the group was welcome at Taylor's house. Jagger remembered how difficult it was to find a place to practice. He said, "Parents were not always very tolerant, but Keith's mum was very tolerant of him playing. Keith was an only child and she didn't have a lot of other distractions, whereas my parents were like 'Get on your homework.' It was a real hard time for me. So I used to go and play with Keith, and then we used to go and play with Dick Taylor. His parents were very tolerant, so we used to go 'round to his house, where we could play louder."[4]

The group was starting to mesh. They were closing in on their own identity. The three musicians had even come up with a name for their band. They called themselves Little Boy Blue and the Blue Boys. They were dedicated to each other and determined to find success. They continued to practice as often as they could.

On November 3, 1960, Jagger came to practice dressed in jeans and winklepickers, which were boots with very long, pointed toes, often worn by rock and rollers. The historic value of that day was not in Jagger's wardrobe but rather in his announcement that he would no longer respond to the name

Mike. Jagger insisted that people address him as Mick—Mick Jagger, a name that is now recognized in almost every corner of the world.[5]

Richards and Jagger practiced their music and visited clubs as often as they could. They couldn't seem to satisfy their need to hear live music. As they listened, their tastes in music grew more refined. Each time they listened to a band, they took pieces away from the experience. Little by little, all the bits of style, rhythm, and beat that they heard from other bands began to collect within themselves. Richards and Jagger were musical sponges and they were about to squeeze out what they had soaked up. What fell from the sponge was a raw and unique musical sound that would eventually captivate huge audiences.

Discovering Jones

In the spring of 1962, Richards and Jagger visited the Ealing Jazz Club in London, England. There they met Brian Jones, who was experimenting with a new style of rock and roll along with keyboard player Ian Stewart. The two musicians called themselves the Rollin' Stones, a title lifted from a song by blues legend Muddy Waters.

Jones's skill on the slide guitar really impressed Richards and Jagger. Richards was very excited about Jones's ability. Richards once said, "Brian was really fantastic, the first person I ever heard playing slide electric guitar. Mick and I both thought he was incredible."[6] Jones mentioned to Jagger and Richards that he wanted to expand his own band. Richards said, "He could have easily joined another group, but he wanted to form his own. The Rolling Stones was Brian's baby."[7] The three musicians did just that; they got together and made a band. Soon after that, the spelling of the band's name, Rollin' Stones, was adjusted and the letter *g* was added. Now calling themselves the Rolling Stones, the band was about to ramp into high gear. The phrase that inspired the original Muddy Waters song says, "a rolling stone gathers no moss." This turned out to be very fitting as a title for the band. The phrase explains that a moving stone or object does not become stale, or stagnant. The Rolling Stones were not a band of musicians that sat and waited for the world to find them. They were enthusiastic about their music and worked hard to bring their sound to as many fans as they could.

The group expanded quickly. With Richards covering lead guitar, Jagger singing lead vocals, Jones on slide guitar, and Taylor on bass guitar, the band was almost complete. Suddenly, an unexpected window of opportunity opened. Jones's former bandmate, Alexis Korner had to cancel his appearance on a BBC radio show. The Rolling Stones were offered the spot. The band snatched up drummer Mick Avory and prepared to hit the airwaves. The Rolling Stones made their first public appearance on July 12, 1962.[8]

The next morning Richards went back home to pack his

bags. After exchanging a few angry words with his parents, he left home for good. Mr. Richards said to his son, "You won't last ten minutes on your own, you bloody layabout."[9] The door slammed and that was that. Richards was gone. Richards moved in with bandmate, Brian Jones. The two spent their first morning together, eating breakfast; cold beans straight from the can.[10]

Blues Buddies Cast Doubt

Meanwhile, Jones was facing criticism from his peers. All the skilled blues and jazz artists that Jones had been playing with greatly respected Jones's talent. They thought he was the next big thing to hit blues. When Jagger and Richards suddenly arrived on the scene, Jones's friends were not impressed. Jones's jazz and blues friends considered Jagger and Richards a couple of untalented showmen who tried to act like musicians. Nevertheless, Jones stood beside his new friends and supported them.

Jones's friends even tried to expose what they felt was Jagger's lack of talent by sabotaging him on stage during a performance. The very well-respected drummer Ginger Baker, along with two other skilled musicians, took the stage one night with Jagger at a club they often played at. What seemed like a fun opportunity for a spontaneous jam session turned out to be a setup to make a fool out of Jagger. In the middle of a song, Baker changed the beat. Jagger, not being a versatile musician at the time, fumbled over his lyrics and couldn't continue the song. It seemed that he was indeed exposed. Instead of walking away from his friend's public humiliation, Jones jumped up onstage and began counting the beats out loud so Jagger could jump back into the groove. It was at that moment that Jones's friends knew that his loyalty to Jagger and Richards was true. Jones was committed to making his new band successful.[11]

Steady Work

The Rolling Stones continued to work, but they hit a stumbling block when Taylor left the band in November 1962. After playing with the Rolling Stones for just a few months, Taylor decided to go back to art school. He was replaced in December by Bill Wyman, who had once played with the Cliftons.

Soon after that, the road to success began to smooth out a bit. The boys found their permanent drummer, Charlie Watts, who officially joined the band in January 1963. That same year the Rolling Stones secured a steady job playing at the Crawdaddy Club. They committed to an eight-month residency and slowly attracted a large following of committed fans. As the band's popularity grew, they picked up contracts with more clubs. Along with the Crawdaddy Club, the Rolling Stones played at the Ken Colyer Club and the Ricky Tick.[12]

Their schedule was packed and it seemed that they were well on their way to success.

The Rolling Stones were doing very well carving out their own path until September 15, 1963, when they found themselves speeding toward fame and fortune. It was on that date that the Rolling Stones opened at the Great Pop Prom, a concert that featured the most popular rock-and-roll band the world had ever seen: the Beatles. The Beatles were taking the world by storm with their brand new style of music. They had just released their fourth hit single, "She Loves You," and were filling concert halls with wild, screaming fans. The Rolling Stones had been given a huge opportunity when asked to play as the opening band for the Beatles. The Rolling Stones did not let their chance at fame slip away. They took the stage dressed for success, wearing dark pants, blue shirts, and black ties. The crowd loved what they heard and the girls went wild over the rebellious-looking, long-haired band members. The show was a huge success and the band earned recognition in popular music magazines such as *Boyfriend* and *Melody Maker.*[13]

Jones Struggles

Even though the Rolling Stones had experienced moments of success, they were still an up-and-coming rock-and-roll band and had to work very hard. Jones, who worked as the band's manager, may have worked harder than any of the other members. Jones overworked his frail body despite his weak state of health. He often worked himself into a state of utter exhaustion. More than once, Jones was found passed out on the floor with his guitar on his lap. There were times he did not make it to rehearsal. Some of the band members began to think Jones didn't care about the band. Resentment toward Jones soon set in. All this responsibility, along with his health problems, proved to be too much for Jones. But because his abusive parents had taught him not to complain, Jones kept his struggles to himself. "I'd rather make a joke of my falling asleep or let them think whatever they would, rather than to let them know the mess my life seemed to be," said Jones.[14]

In November 1963, just two months after opening for the Beatles, the Rolling Stones set out on a tour of the United Kingdom as a headlining band. They had finally pulled themselves out of the local scene and were now considered to have hit the big time. The band was making enough money to support itself. Their schedule was full, and it seemed that the hard part was over.

Conflict Heats Up

Although the Rolling Stones seemed to be on the right track, conflict waited around the corner. Jones's seemingly lazy behavior continued and he began to lose the respect of his bandmates. Unfortunately for Jones, a record producer named Andrew Oldham stepped onto the scene with new ideas at a time when some of the members of the Rolling Stones were starting to think about finding a new manager. Oldham began to take notice of the Rolling Stones. He had his own ideas for the band and started to take control. Oldham wanted the Rolling Stones to take on the image of a rebellious and gritty bunch of rockers while Jones wanted to keep the band's focus on rhythm and blues. Oldham started a conflict between the members of the Rolling Stones when he told them that Jones had been taking money from the group. Jones denied Oldham's claims but the band became divided over the incident. Little by little, the band began to follow Oldham's vision more than Jones's. Oldham's scheme to take over the band seemed to be working. The Rolling Stones signed their first record deal with Decca Records soon after Oldham's involvement with the band.

Oldham's control of the band grew stronger and Jones was forced to take a secondary role in making decisions for the band. Oldham removed keyboard player Stewart from the official lineup and placed more emphasis on Jagger and Richards, forcing Jones farther and farther into the background. The band's schedule was filled with tours and recording sessions. In January 1964, the band kicked off a twenty-nine-day British tour. Even with this busy schedule, the guys still drove themselves to shows and were responsible for loading, unloading, and setting up their own equipment. They continued to behave as unruly rebels, often causing chaos to erupt from fans. Many times the Rolling Stones had a difficult time finding a place to stay. Hotels refused to let them rent rooms for fear of the destruction the band might cause.

Oldham encouraged the Rolling Stones to continue to act like wild rock stars. The fans started to go crazy. Heavy security was needed to protect band members as fans swarmed them. One fan ripped the shirt right off Jagger's back and even the pants off Watts, right on stage while he played

EXCITED FANS ARE HELD BACK BY POLICE OFFICERS IN NEW YORK IN JUNE 1964.

the drums![15] Jones, who was fearful of the crowds, referred to the fans as "the flesh eaters."[16]

Growing Success

The band continued to tour, and as it did its popularity grew. As the Stones became more popular, their income increased. The band began riding to shows in the backs of limousines, and roadies, or crew members, loaded and unloaded its equipment. The Stones toured the United States and ended with a performance in New York City at the world-famous concert venue Radio City Music Hall. The band formed a company called Rolling Stones Limited, which produced such merchandise as T-shirts, posters, and photographs. The Rolling Stones had become a huge band, known all over the world.

Over the next five years, the Rolling Stones kept doing what they did best. They played to thousands of fans and released new records. In 1964 the Rolling Stones released the hit singles "It's All Over Now" and "Time Is on My Side." The following year the band put out two of its biggest hits, "The Last Time" and "(I Can't Get No) Satisfaction." In 1966 they released two experimental pieces, "Under My Thumb" and "Lady Jane." These two songs used two instruments, the marimba and the dulcimer, which were not typically heard in rock-and-roll music. That same year they hit a major milestone when their song "Paint It, Black" reached number one on the record charts.[17]

Trouble With the Law

The band's stretch of good luck came to a halt when Jagger and Richards were arrested for possession of illegal drugs. In February 1967, police raided a party being held at Richards's home. Officials searched Jagger and found a small amount of amphetamine pills commonly known as "speed" or "pep pills." Jagger was cited with drug possession while Richards was charged with allowing the substance to be consumed in his home. On May 9, the same day Richards and Jagger received their sentences for the drug incident, Jones faced his own drug-related problems. Police raided his home and found the drug, cannabis, also known as pot or marijuana. Jones was arrested and charged with possession of illegal drugs. The arrest didn't stop Jones from using drugs. He was arrested the following year on the same charge.

All three band members were convicted of their crimes. Jagger and Richards were sentenced to jail but never spent time behind bars. Controversy added to the drama of Jagger's and Richards's sentences. Their lawyers claimed that the men were unfairly targeted simply because they happened to be celebrities. They argued that common citizens would not be treated so harshly on a drug possession of such a small scale. The attorneys representing Jagger and Richards were able to

Mick Jagger (left) and Keith Richards leave a court in England in October 1967 after being arrested on drug charges.

overturn their sentences. Jones, on the other hand, was not let off so easily. He was sentenced to three years of probation.

Drug use within the band continued. Although Jagger and Richards were able to avoid the police, Jones was arrested again the next year. Once again Jones was found in possession of cannabis. Most people who knew Jones were not surprised. His regular use of alcohol, speed, and marijuana was no secret to his friends. Soon those who cared about Jones would realize how serious his drug problem really was.

After Jones's second arrest, tensions between the band members increased. Jagger and Jones did not get along well at all during 1967. Jones's drug habits began to spiral out of control. Jagger had a different vision for the Rolling Stones than Jones did. It seemed that their arguments could no longer be resolved.

Despite their differences, the Rolling Stones continued to play. Fans heard rumors of disagreements between band members, but as long as the boys kept playing rock and roll, the fans didn't concern themselves with the personal lives of the band. The Rolling Stones had become a moneymaking music machine that perhaps needed a tune-up, but nevertheless kept playing.

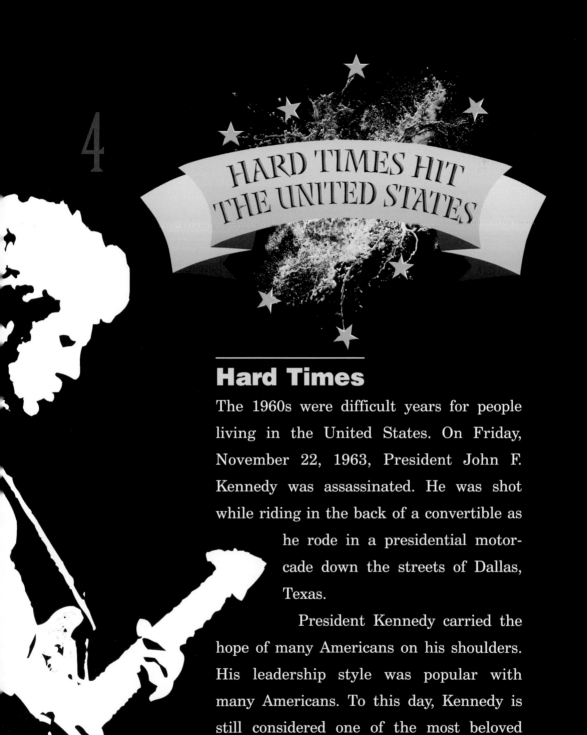

HARD TIMES HIT THE UNITED STATES

4

Hard Times

The 1960s were difficult years for people living in the United States. On Friday, November 22, 1963, President John F. Kennedy was assassinated. He was shot while riding in the back of a convertible as he rode in a presidential motorcade down the streets of Dallas, Texas.

President Kennedy carried the hope of many Americans on his shoulders. His leadership style was popular with many Americans. To this day, Kennedy is still considered one of the most beloved presidents of all time. The violent attack on the president sent shockwaves through the country. Sadness quickly spread over the land.[1]

Going to War

The assassination of the president was not the only challenge the United States endured during the 1960s. The country was also involved in a new war with Vietnam. At that time, much of the world feared the spread of a type of government called Communism. Under Communism, individuals do not own property like they do in the United States. In a Communist government the entire community controls the property. This may sound like a fair way to live, but in reality Communist governments are usually ruled by small groups of leaders who treat the rest of the community unfairly. Communist leaders throughout history have been extremely authoritative and have taken freedoms away from their citizens. Many have fought ruthlessly to keep their power.[2]

The world watched as North and South Vietnam went to war. North Vietnam wanted to rule with a Communist government and South Vietnam wanted to remain free. The United States joined the war in 1965. The decision to join the war was made in order to prevent the spread of Communism. It was a long and difficult war that many Americans protested. The United States was divided between people who supported the war and people who did not. Many protesters held rallies to voice their opinions against the war. Finally, after ten years of fighting, the United States left Vietnam. North Vietnam won control over South Vietnam and the country became unified as a Communist nation.

More than fifty-eight thousand Americans were killed during the conflict. Three hundred four thousand were wounded. Many soldiers lost limbs and even more returned home haunted by the horrible memories of the war. In 1961, before the United States joined the war, President Kennedy said, "Let every nation know, whether it wishes us well or ill, that we shall pay any price, bear any burden, meet any hardship, support any friend, oppose any foe, in order to assure the survival of liberty."[3] His words rang true. The Vietnam War was the longest military conflict in United States history.

The tragic events of the 1960s left Americans desperate for happiness. American teens were growing particularly restless. For many, music provided the escape they needed.

The Beatles Arrive

Just seventy-seven days after the assassination of President Kennedy, the Beatles left their home in Liverpool, England, and arrived in the United States. On February 7, 1964, the Beatles stepped out of their airplane and into New York City. From that day forward, the music scene in the United States would never be the same.[4]

The Beatles brought with them a rebellious sound, something teens always seem to connect with. After looking back on their early success in the United States, Beatles band member John Lennon said, "The thing is, in America, it just seemed ridiculous—I mean, the idea of having a hit record over there, it was just something you could never do."[5]

The Beatles did more than score a hit record. Forty-five of the band's songs hit the Top 40 in record sales during the next six years. Twenty Beatles tunes reached the number-one slot in the United States. In 1964 the band set a record when five Beatles songs filled the first five slots on Billboard's Top Pop Singles chart.[6] The Beatles still hold the record for highest album sales. They have sold more than 106 million albums in the United States alone.[7]

The Beatles were more popular than any band the world had ever seen. Swarms of screaming fans greeted the Beatles at airports. Hordes of teenage girls chased them down alleys and waited for them outside hotels, hoping for a quick glimpse of their favorite band. "Beatlemania," the term invented to describe the craze, had taken the United States by storm.

The British Invasion

More bands would soon follow the Beatles. The frenzy of rock-and-roll fans had plenty of bands to chase. The British Invasion was about to fall upon the United States.

The British Invasion refers to a wave of rock-and-roll bands that came from England and found great success in the United States. The Beatles are credited with being the band to stimulate the invasion. Several bands that also made huge impacts on the American music scene followed them. Bands

such as the Kinks, the Who, and the Rolling Stones brought an even more rebellious sound to the United States than the Beatles had. Music fans were ready to rock and overall record sales skyrocketed.

Although the Beatles played rock and roll, their sound was still a bit clean compared to the sounds of the Kinks, the Who, and the Rolling Stones. The Kinks played their own style of rock and roll. They combined the steady rhythms heard mostly in blues music with the gravelly voice of the lead singer, Ray Davies. Their first hit, "You Really Got Me," is still considered one of rock and roll's all-time greatest hits.[8]

The Who invaded the United States in the middle of 1967. The band had already earned a reputation for being wild and destructive, especially on stage. Pete Townshend, lead guitarist for the Who, smashed his guitar to splinters onstage for the first time in 1965. He was playing at a club

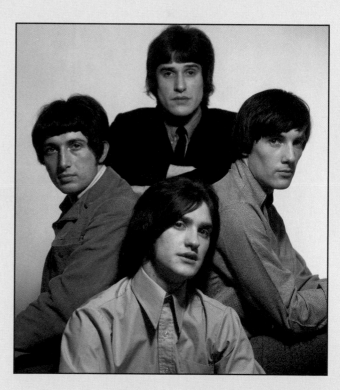

THE KINKS IN THE 1960s

called the Railway Hotel in Harrow, England, when he accidentally broke his guitar while playing it. Frustration took hold of Townshend, and with wild aggression he smashed the instrument to smithereens. Rather than being afraid or put off by Townshend's display of anger, the audience cheered. Smashing guitars soon became Townshend's trademark and a highlight of many of the Who's stage shows.[9]

The showing of raw emotion on stage was particularly appealing to teens in the United States. The Who provided frustrated youth with an outlet for their caged anger. Record sales reflected the band's appeal. "My Generation," "I Can't Explain," "Who Are You?" and "Substitute" are just some of the hit song titles that came from the Who. Their creative mix of rebellion with rhythm and blues proved to be a sound that still appeals to the masses.

The Rolling Stones were also part of the British Invasion. They are often listed along with the Kinks and the Who as one of the most influential bands in rock-and-roll history. The appeal of these bands was their raw and gritty sound, a sound that was unique to rock and roll.

The Birth of Rock and Roll

The genre of music called blues is often thought of as the backbone of rock and roll. Blues is a style of music that grew out of sadness, depression, and the struggle to survive. Blues sprouted in part from the songs sung by African slaves who were forced to live in horrible conditions on large farms called plantations in the American South. While being whipped to work harder, slaves sang of their hardships while harvesting cotton in the slave owners fields. Most historians agree that the genre that we now recognize as blues was first played in the North Mississippi Delta. The music played there was a mix of African-American spiritual hymns and field hollers. When singing work songs, one lead worker would lay down a chant, and in return the group of workers would echo both the tune and the lyrics. Work songs and field hollers laid the foundation for what is now recognized as blues. While the sound of the music changed greatly over time, the call and echo technique is still the backbone of blues. In traditional blues, the singer also lays down, or sings, the melody. The singer then echoes the melody with his guitar and or his voice. The lyrics are repetitious and tell of a variety of hardships, from working hard to not having enough food to eat. But one important difference from work songs is that blues is now most often sung during times of leisure.

The first official blues recording was made in 1895 by George W. Johnson when he performed the song, "Laughing Song." Years later, blues began to gain popularity when W. C. Handy released "Memphis Blues" and "St. Louis Blues" between 1910 and 1915. These two songs slowly pushed blues north as more African Americans began to catch on to the sound. By the 1920s, blues had gained national popularity.[10]

Even though blues was increasing in popularity, most white Americans refused to listen to it. These Americans were still caught in the racial divide and did not open their minds to the African-American culture.[11]

In the United Kingdom, people seemed to be more open to accepting other cultures. During the late 1950s and early 1960s, listeners in the United Kingdom began to catch on to the driving beat of blues music. When the teenage population discovered the trend, they snatched onto the sound of blues and twisted it into something of their own. Young musicians began experimenting with combinations of blues, jazz, country, and pop. The music that emerged was rock and roll. Muddy Waters, a cherished blues artist, emphasized the connection of the blues to rock and roll with his song "The Blues Had a Baby and They Named it Rock and Roll."[12]

The roots of rock and roll grew out of sorrow and hardship. Knowing the

MUDDY WATERS IN THE 1950s

history of rock and roll, one can understand how the sound was often very appealing to teens and even adults who were living in the difficult times that the United States faced in the 1960s. It was during that decade that rock and roll took hold of the country. After the assassination of President Kennedy, the country's involvement in the Vietnam War, and the British Invasion, rock and roll had a firm grip on the youth of the United States. Even today rock and roll continues to hold strong.

The Rolling Stones in 1969

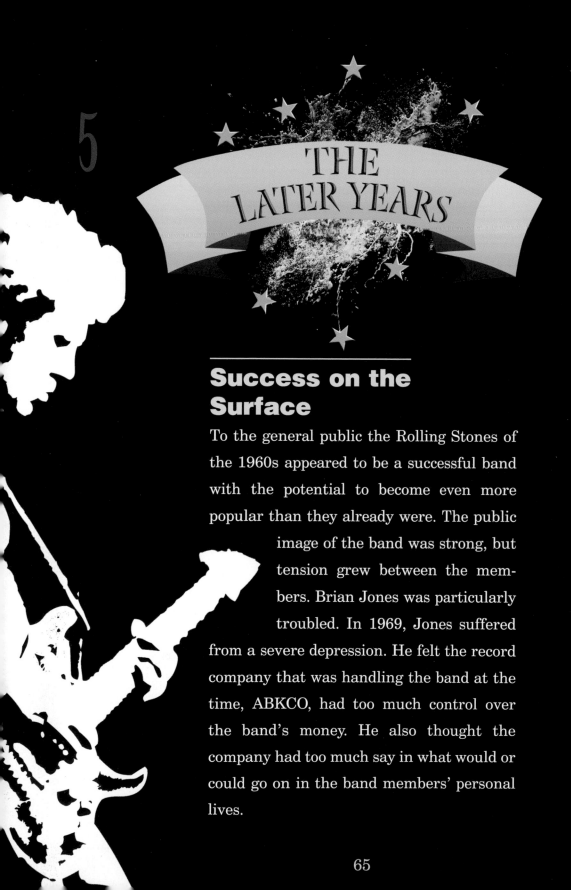

THE LATER YEARS

Success on the Surface

To the general public the Rolling Stones of the 1960s appeared to be a successful band with the potential to become even more popular than they already were. The public image of the band was strong, but tension grew between the members. Brian Jones was particularly troubled. In 1969, Jones suffered from a severe depression. He felt the record company that was handling the band at the time, ABKCO, had too much control over the band's money. He also thought the company had too much say in what would or could go on in the band members' personal lives.

"Most musicians don't understand that they're captured by the industry, but they are. They become products of the money machine and when I understood what was taking place, I refused to be part of it," said Jones.[1]

Jones felt trapped in his own home. He was certain that the men he hired to make household repairs were actually working for the record company. Jones believed the men were assigned to keep him isolated from the outside world. Jones accused the men of disconnecting his phone, stealing every scrap of his food, and hiding his personal property. Living under these conditions, Jones's depression became worse.

Jones's estate was named Cotchford and was formerly owned by A. A. Milne, the creator of Winnie-the-Pooh. Jones purchased the home hoping to find tranquility in the atmosphere left behind by the creative children's book author. But Jones painted an unhappy picture when he described his home, "Cotchford felt almost like a burial ground at times. To suddenly not have any fans surrounding me made me feel dead inside."[2]

Jones Slips Away

Jones also felt the other members of the Rolling Stones pulling away from him. They had found success and it was pulling them into new and unexpected directions. The band had taken on a life of its own. The other members had a different musical focus than Jones. They wanted to have the freedom to experiment with mixing the Stones' sound with other genres such as disco and psychedelic rock. Jones had a very specific vision for the band and he felt the other members were pushing the group away from its original blues-based rock and roll. Jones was in a slump. His creative energy had been drained. The Rolling Stones began to talk about firing Jones.

Jones once said, "I have this niggling feeling that maybe I've lost my edge. . . . Of course, they told me I already did lose it . . . the band has told me, management has told me. Even the news headlines."[3] He went on to say, "I was an outcast and am an outcast. . . . I'm not part of my own band any longer." At this point, Jones was still technically a member of the Rolling Stones, but that would soon change.

Jones never pulled out of his depression. Jones tried everything he could to feel happy again. He started having more frequent wild parties at his estate. Unfortunately Jones reached for alcohol to numb the pain in his life. He was spiraling out of control.

Powerful arguments erupted between Jones, the rest of the band, and the record company. Jones, who was the founding member of the Rolling Stones, wanted to break away and start a new band with the same name. He wanted the rest of the band to pay him for the creative work he had done and let him move on, free to create with a new group of musicians.

A Tragic End

Jones's break with the Rolling Stones ended on June 8, 1969.[4] Mick Jagger, Keith Richards, and Charlie Watts all paid a visit to Jones at his country estate. According to Jones, the three demanded that Jones return all legal rights to the songs he had written as well as the rights to the Rolling Stones name. Jones protested angrily, but in the end the rest of the band took control of everything. Jones was now truly alone. His band had united and was working together to push him out. Jagger finally said to Jones, "This is the way it's going to be, Brian. We're going on without you."[5]

The decision pushed Jones over the edge. On July 3, 1969, Jones was found dead at the bottom of his own swimming pool. Although the official report labeled his death as "death by misadventure" there are some people who wonder if there was more to the story. Some say he drowned after losing consciousness after taking a mixture of alcohol and sleeping pills. Others say he committed suicide. While the details of the end of Jones's life are a mystery, there is no doubt that his life was filled with hardship and his story ended in sad tragedy. During a concert held soon after Jones's death, Jagger opened the show with a eulogy for Jones. After his words of respect, thousands of butterflies were released as a symbol of Jones's free spirit.[6]

Years later Jagger commented on Jones in an interview with *Rolling Stone* magazine. Jagger said, "The thing about

Brian is that he was an extremely difficult person. There was something very, very disturbed about him. He was very unhappy with life, very frustrated. He was very talented, but he had a very paranoid personality and [was] not at all suited to be in show business."[7]

The Band Moves On

Jones was replaced by the Stones' old friend and guitarist Mick Taylor. With Taylor ready to rock, the Rolling Stones returned to the music scene with wild energy. The Stones put out many songs between 1967 and 1968. Many of the singles put out during that time became classic rock hits. "Jumpin' Jack Flash," "Street Fighting Man," and "Midnight Rambler" are three examples.

During this time, witchcraft, satanism, and violence intrigued the band and the music they played began to reflect its fascination. The album titled *Their Satanic Majesties Request* was released in 1967. This album is often described as an experimental collection with a dark, psychedelic tone. Some Christian groups claimed that songs like "Sing This All Together" and "2000 Light Years From Home" were written to cause listeners to fall into the grips of satanic worship. The song "Sympathy for the Devil," a single from the 1968 album *Beggars Banquet,* caused the Christian community to seriously question the Rolling Stones' intentions. The song's lyrics are written as if Jagger were actually Satan, as he addresses himself as Lucifer, a name often given to the Devil.

In addition to witchcraft, the Rolling Stones produced a collection of songs containing lyrics that described violence, murder, and chaos. "Midnight Rambler" and "Hand of Fate" are two examples of songs that describe particularly violent scenes. Fans were excited and energized by the rebellion spearheaded by the band. Many of those fans were fed up by the violence of the Vietnam War. The expressions in these songs seemed to offer a release for feelings of frustration for some fans. The Stones began to attract a base of fans that reached far beyond that of the swarms of screaming girls and young teenage boys that once filled concert venues. Fans with a history of violence started joining the audience.

Rock and Roll's Worst Day

The violence peaked on December 6, 1969, a day often described as "rock and roll's worst day." It was on that day that the Rolling Stones played a concert at Altamont Speedway just outside San Francisco, California.[8]

The Rolling Stones had decided to hold a free concert. The concert's list of bands included groups such as Jefferson Airplane and Crosby, Stills, Nash, and Young. The Rolling Stones were listed as the main act and were also the primary force behind planning the event. While making plans, the Rolling Stones decided to hire the Hells Angels, a motorcycle

The Rolling Stones performed at the Altamont Speedway on December 6, 1969.

gang, to cover security and crowd control. That decision proved to be a devastating mistake. As the crowd of four hundred thousand swarmed the speedway, the Hells Angels stepped in with fists, guns, and knives.[9] Many fans were injured during fights with members of the Hells Angels. Reports claim that more than two hundred fans were hurt during the chaos.

At the end of the day, the Rolling Stones were ready to take the stage. Jagger tried his best to calm the crowd. He spoke to his fans and said, "Sisters . . . brothers . . . Come on now. That means everybody cool out. Just be cool now, come on."[10] Richards also stepped up and shouted at the crowd, "Either those cats cool it, or we don't play." The threat of the Rolling Stones walking off the stage seemed to calm the audience down, at least long enough for the band to begin. The band played a few mellow tunes to help subdue the crowd. Then they pulled out one of their big hits, "Under My Thumb."

A few seconds into the song, complete chaos broke loose in the crowd. Just steps away from the stage, the Hells Angels started to harass a fan named Meredith Hunter. Reports say the fight broke out suddenly. A gun was drawn. A knife was drawn. Hunter went down and the Hells Angels swarmed around him. Tragically, Hunter was stabbed by a member of the gang and killed.[11]

After the horrible incident, Altamont was closed to all

rock-and-roll events. Years later Jagger commented on the incident in an interview. "[I felt] awful," said Jagger. "I mean, just awful. You feel a responsibility. How could it all have been so silly and wrong? It was more how awful it was to have had this experience and how awful it was for someone to get killed and how sad it was for his family."[12]

Time to Think

After the concert the Rolling Stones returned home. They took some time to rethink what direction they wanted the band to take. During the early 1970s, the Rolling Stones made some big business decisions. They decided not to renew their record contract with their current producer, Decca, and moved to Atlantic Records. The Rolling Stones also fired their manager, Andrew Oldham, who they accused of stealing money from the band. They also replaced their tour manager. Jagger even ended his relationship with his longtime girlfriend Marianne Faithfull.

During this time of transition, Taylor began to feel underappreciated by the rest of the band. He wanted to have more creative input. He wanted credit for his songwriting. He wanted freedom to express himself as a musician. Taylor didn't see a way to get what he really wanted out of the Rolling Stones. One night in 1974, at a party held at Richards's house, Taylor sat on the couch between Jagger and another musician friend, Ronnie Wood. Taylor leaned over to Jagger and said

MICK JAGGER (LEFT) AND RONNIE WOOD IN 1977

very simply, "I'm leaving the group."[13] Taylor stood up, left the party, and left the Rolling Stones.

Wood and Jagger were left sitting on the couch, feeling a bit stunned. Jagger knew Wood was an excellent guitar player so he suggested that Wood take Taylor's place. Wood responded by saying, "Of course I would, except I'm with the Faces and I can't let them down. I don't want to split them up."[14]

Jagger replied, "I don't want to split up the Faces either, but if I get desperate can I ring you?"[15]

New Guitarist

Several months later, Jagger called Wood. "I'm really desperate, can you help us out?"[16] Jagger asked. Wood agreed. He went to audition for the job but was a bit surprised that the band was looking at other guitarists as well. One of those guitarists was the legendary Eric Clapton. Clapton said to Wood, "I'm a much better guitarist than you." Wood responded, "I know that, but you've gotta live with these guys as well as play with them. There's no way you can do that."[17]

In the end, Wood was offered the job. The Rolling Stones made the right choice, as Wood still remains with the band today. After more than thirty years, Wood has managed to play and "live with the guys" through many rock-and-roll adventures.

The Stones continued to make music in the 1970s. They put out several albums: *Goats Head Soup; Sticky Fingers,* which contained the huge hit "Brown Sugar"; *It's Only Rock 'N Roll; Exile on Main St.,* which was a collection of tunes recorded between 1968 and 1972; and *Black and Blue.* While their work was still popular, many critics felt that this string of albums did not compare to the band's earlier works. Many fans felt that the band had hit a creative slump.

Even though their momentum was not what it once was, the Rolling Stones pulled through the 1970s and emerged in the 1980s with new energy. Their best-selling album ever, *Tattoo You,* stayed at number one for over nine weeks.

MICK JAGGER (LEFT) AND KEITH RICHARDS PERFORM
AT A CONCERT IN PHILADELPHIA, PENNSYLVANIA, IN
SEPTEMBER 1981.

Later in the decade, the Rolling Stones released the album *Steel Wheels*, which was complimented by most critics as showcasing both creative and solid music. Aside from reports of quarreling between Jagger and Richards, the 1980s were good to the Rolling Stones.[18] In 1989 the Rolling Stones were inducted into the Rock and Roll Hall of Fame. This event put the finishing touch on yet another successful decade.

Wyman Retires

With the 1980s under their belts, the Rolling Stones faced the 1990s. Bass guitar player Bill Wyman decided to leave the band while it was at the top of the charts. He announced his retirement in 1992. The band never officially replaced Wyman. Instead it toured as Jagger, Richards, Watts, and Wood.

The 1990s also gave the band members time to pursue solo projects. Watts put out a couple of jazz albums. Wood continued with his solo projects and released his fifth album, *Slide on This*. Richards packed his bags for a short tour following his solo release of *Main Offender*. Jagger sold more than 2 million copies of his solo album *Wandering Spirit*.

The end of the century brought the members of the Rolling Stones a chance to experiment on their own. They each took time to pursue individual adventures. Luckily for their fans, the band reunited just in time to take the new millennium by storm.

6

WHERE ARE THEY NOW?

A Long Journey

The Rolling Stones have come a long way. They have proved to be a popular band with both older generations and with young music lovers, and continue to be today. With more than forty years of performing and recording experience before the turn of the century, the Rolling Stones are a band with more rock-and-roll history than any other act. With a touring schedule that has taken them around the world many times, the members of the Rolling Stones are global citizens. Their now wrinkled and well-worn faces are some of the most recognizable of any celebrities in the world. Unlike some rock-and-roll stars who slowed down in their later years, the Rolling Stones are still a very active and popular band.

Charity Concerts

Even as he passed his sixtieth birthday, Mick Jagger and the rest of his aging bandmates brought in the new millennium with energy and enthusiasm. The band seemed determined to quench the thirst for new music and live performances that its fans so desired. The band's most significant performance of 2001 may have been in the Concert for New York City. The concert was held in response to the tragic attacks experienced in the United States on September 11, 2001. On that day, the United States was overcome with fear and sadness after terrorists sent jet airplanes crashing into the World Trade Center buildings in New York City and into the Pentagon in Washington D.C.

The Concert for New York City was staged in New York's Madison Square Garden. The musicians who played there did so in honor of the many people killed during the attacks. Special recognition was given to firefighters and policemen, as they were the first to respond during the emergency. Artists Paul McCartney, the Who, Eric Clapton, Jagger, and Keith Richards are examples of some of the dozens of musicians who gave the gift of music to the survivors on October 20, 2001. The event raised more than 30 million dollars to help victims of the terrorist attacks and their families.[1] During the concert,

Richards took the stage and said, "I got a feeling this town's gonna make it," before singing "Salt of the Earth," a song that pays tribute to hardworking, common people.[2]

In 2002, the Rolling Stones visited nearly eighty cities during the Licks Tour, which ended in November 2003.[3] As part of the Licks Tour, the Rolling Stones stopped in Toronto, Canada, to join the Molson Canadian Rocks for Toronto concert. The concert was a benefit event supporting their Canadian fans who had suffered from an outbreak of a disease called SARS. SARS is a very contagious respiratory

THE ROLLING STONES PERFORMED IN A BENEFIT CONCERT IN 2003 AGAINST SARS.

disease that is passed easily from one person to another. When SARS spread through Toronto, a city with a population of almost 3 million, more than one hundred forty people contracted the disease and twenty-three of those patients died.[4] Despite the fairly low death count, the disease spread fear across the country and Toronto suffered from economic decline as tourists and visitors stayed away from the city.

A reported four hundred ninety thousand fans showed up to watch musicians such as AC/DC, Rush, the Guess Who, and Justin Timberlake.[5] Fans who attended the concert were encouraged to write messages of well-wishing and support on two removable walls that were erected just for the event. After the concert the walls were disassembled and donated to the city of Toronto.[6] The Rolling Stones continued their support of SARS victims in Hong Kong when they participated in a similar concert during November 2003. Both concerts were wildly successful and attracted an amazing number of fans. When describing the concert scene in Toronto, reporter Jenny Wells of CTV News said, "The Guess Who was saying this is the first time they've ever seen the horizon meet a sea of heads." Jagger responded by saying, "This is nothing like we've ever seen before. It's a fantastic buzz."[7]

Still Working Hard

Only two years later the Rolling Stones launched A Bigger Bang Tour in 2005. This tour, which supported the band's new album with the same name, sent Jagger, Richards, Charlie Watts, and Ronnie Wood skipping across continents. They traveled to North America, South America, and East Asia.

The band made a pit-stop performance during the middle of its tour. On February 5, 2006, the Rolling Stones played the halftime show during the Super Bowl football game held in Detroit, Michigan. The Rolling Stones played on a stage built in the shape of their famous lip and tongue logo. As Jagger began singing "Start Me Up" the fabric sheet that formed the tongue was removed, revealing a hive of wired fans who jumped, clapped, and screamed throughout the exciting performance.

After the Super Bowl show the Rolling Stones experienced a few setbacks. In April 2006, Richards reportedly fell from a coconut tree while he vacationed in Fiji and cracked his skull. Days after the incident, Richards was hospitalized and underwent observation to make sure the injury wasn't more serious than first assumed.[8]

In June of that same year, guitarist Wood checked himself into a rehabilitation center to help him control his abuse of alcohol. The *Sun* reported that a source said, "Ronnie has fought a long battle with drink. He has started drinking again over the last few weeks and it has got out of control. Worrying about his mate, Keith, has not helped."[9] Wood stayed in rehab for one month. He quickly reunited with the Rolling Stones and they hit the concert circuit again.

After a bit of a rough year, the Rolling Stones were back in business once again. A Bigger Bang Tour continued through 2007, when the band enjoyed performing in several cities throughout Europe. When it was over, A Bigger Bang Tour had brought in more money than any tour ever performed by a rock-and-roll band. The Guinness Book of World Records reports the tour grossed a total of $437 million, a world record that may stand for a very long time.

On the Big Screen

The Rolling Stones participated in an interesting project in 2008. Well-known film director Martin Scorsese wanted to produce a documentary about the band. He approached the Rolling Stones and asked if he could film them live while playing at the intimate Beacon Theater in New York. The concert was held as a benefit by the Clinton Foundation to help raise money for the foundation's many charities.

Even though the Rolling Stones do not enjoy playing on stage with cameras in the way, they agreed to work with Scorsese. The end result of their collaboration was a documentary film called *Shine a Light*. The movie was marketed as a chance for fans to see the Rolling Stones up close, on the big screen, as they performed in an amazing setting. The film included clips from historical interviews with the Rolling Stones as well as shots of behind-the-scenes activity. Footage of President Bill Clinton and his family greeting the Rolling

Stones adds a bit of humor to the scene. The pre-concert activity is put on hold as the band is asked to wait for Hillary Clinton's mother, who was anxious to meet the band, to arrive. When she arrives, Mrs. Clinton says, "Hi Mom. The Rolling Stones have been waiting for *you*!"[10]

After fulfilling their obligations to the Clintons, the Rolling Stones are ready to get up in front of their fans. The concert starts off with a bright flash of lights and a guitar riff by Richards. Seconds later Jagger rushes onstage and begins singing one of the band's biggest hits, "Jumpin' Jack Flash."

Many fans traveled to IMAX theaters, which are theaters with very large screens, to watch the film. One fan said, "It was definitely a terrific concert experience. The Stones blew the audience's mind with their performance."[11]

Although the Rolling Stones did have to adjust to performing around the film crew, they enjoyed playing with noteworthy musicians who stepped on stage as guest performers. Christina Aguilera, Buddy Guy, and Jack White all joined the Rolling Stones for special performances during the concert.

The *Shine a Light* project was a film that involved the collaboration of the entire band. But each member of the Rolling Stones has his own list of accomplishments and personal interests, too. Richards worked alongside actor Johnny Depp during the creation of the 2007 blockbuster pirate film, *Pirates of the Caribbean: At World's End*, the third in the

IN 2007, KEITH RICHARDS (LEFT) PLAYED CAPTAIN TEAGUE IN *PIRATES OF THE CARIBBEAN: AT WORLD'S END.*

series. In the film, Richards plays Captain Teague, the father of Depp's character. The casting is amusing as Depp admits that he used Richards's persona as his inspiration when creating his own character, Captain Jack Sparrow, the legendary but sometimes bumbling lead pirate from the *Pirates* films.

When asked if he thought being pirate-like was helpful in surviving the music industry, Richards said, "[The music business is] like a pool of piranhas. You want to get in there? You better not be tasty."[12]

Personal Interests

For Richards, acting is nothing more than a hobby, or something unusual to do to pass the time. Richards has another hobby that is not so surprising: He collects guitars. His collection holds more than three thousand instruments. Many of the guitars were gifts given to him, and others he purchased himself. Because he has so many, Richards is considering putting the collection on display in a museum. "I've probably got too many. I have 3,000 guitars and only one pair of hands. It's an incredible collection of musical instruments but I only play about ten of them, and guitars have to be played."[13]

Richards has started giving some of his guitars away as gifts. He gave one guitar to musician Buddy Guy after he took the stage with the Rolling Stones during the *Shine a Light* concert. "I thought, this is my respect to Buddy and to Muddy Waters and all the other guys who [inspired me]," said Richards about the exchange.[14]

It is no surprise that Richards likes guitars. But many people are surprised to find out that he is an enthusiastic reader. According to Richards, when he isn't on tour, kicking back with a good book is one of his favorite pastimes. Richards once said, "I tell you what I do when I'm not working with the Stones, I kick back, baby. . . . I've read every book ever written.

I'm running out. Somebody please write one!"[15] While his statement is most likely an exaggeration, Richards obviously has a passion for reading.

Making Movies

While Richards has a passion for reading, Jagger has a passion for movies, so much so that in 1995, Jagger founded Jagged Films, a production company that creates feature-length films. Even though it was founded in the mid-1990s, the company did not start releasing mass-market films until 2001. Set in World War II, the film *Enigma* presents a mysterious plot of suspense as the characters race to break a secret code.[16] In 2008 Jagged Films released the film *The Women,* which is a remake of a 1939 film with the same title. The film boasts stars such as Meg Ryan and Annette Bening and explores the friendships between a group of high-society women living in New York City.[17]

Jagger himself earned a significant nod from British high society. On December 12, 2003, Jagger was granted knighthood by Prince Charles. From that day forward, Jagger's official title is Sir Michael (Mick) Jagger. The honor did not prompt fellow bandmate Richards to congratulate Jagger. Instead Richards reacted with disbelief and disappointment. "I told Mike it's a paltry honor. . . . It's not what the Stones is about, is it?" said Richards.[18]

Jagger simply said of the honor, "I didn't expect to get one. I just didn't."[19]

Knight or not, Jagger still continues his act as a purebred rock star. Faithful fans rest assured that Jagger's title of "Sir" has not softened his edgy personality.

Musical Interests Stretch Beyond the Band

The one band member who does seem to have a more refined personality is drummer Watts. His cool demeanor behind the drum kit quickly became his trademark. At first glance, one might assume Watts would be better suited playing for a hip jazz act. In fact, Watts spends a great deal of time fostering his love of jazz. He has played with a big band group called the Charlie Watts Orchestra. The band played big band style jazz which features trumpets, saxophones, trombones, clarinets, and drums. Watts also worked with his friend Jim Keltner in creating a techno/instrumental album filled with unusual modern sounds. Released in 2000, the album *Charlie Watts/ Jim Keltner Project* introduced listeners to a wide range of sounds influenced by African as well as Indian music.[20]

Watts's most recent jazz recording was taped live at the famous Ronnie Scott's Jazz Club in London, England. Released on August 24, 2004, the album showcases the big band sound and has gained compliments from music critics. Watts realizes that his jazz career will never bring home a paycheck that can begin to compare to that earned with the Stones, but he truly enjoys playing jazz. Watts once said, "Nobody ever buys these things, but they're lovely to do, and they give me a chance to play in a totally different way to how I do in the Stones."[21]

Watts was diagnosed with throat cancer in 2004 but has since made a full recovery. His triumph over the disease was reinforced in 2006 with the joyful recognition of being named into the Drummer Hall of Fame by *Modern Drummer* magazine. Now Watts spends his time enjoying life on his six-hundred-acre ranch where he raises Arabian horses with his wife, Shirley.[22]

Gallery Artist

Wood has interests outside the Rolling Stones, too. Wood is a talented painter who has painted portraits of famous pop icons such as actor Jack Nicholson, musician Jim Morrison, and comedian Jim Belushi. He also enjoys painting wildlife. His paintings of apes, panthers, and other exotic animals have helped raise money to promote wildlife conservation, a cause that is close to Wood's heart.

Wood attended the Ealing Art College before he began playing the guitar. His works have been featured in galleries in countries such as Japan, Great Britain, and the United States.[23]

Painting is a joy that Wood cannot put to rest, even while touring with the Rolling Stones. Wood said that while on tour,

The Rolling Stones were in Martin Scorsese's *Shine a Light* documentary. From left to right: Mick Jagger, Ronnie Wood, Keith Richards, and Charlie Watts.

"During rehearsals, I draw up the set lists on big canvases. . . . We hang these set lists on the rehearsal room walls. . . . I illustrate them, sometimes Keith and Mick add little doodles and they become works of art in their own right."[24]

Wood's growth as an artist started to really take off in the early 2000s. In 2003 Wood showed his work at a gallery in New York City and then again in Japan. "The Americans were so welcoming and appreciative of my work. And although I have no idea where they all came from, 5,000 people showed up at an exhibition of my paintings at a gallery in Osaka, Japan."[25] Wood's paintings sell for tens of thousands of dollars. He has even had a painting list for $140,000, too expensive even for bandmate Jagger's taste.[26]

Most people recognize the members of the Rolling Stones only as rock-and-roll musicians. But their interests are numerous and varied. From acting, to painting, to breeding world-class horses, the men who make up the Rolling Stones are rich in talent that stretches outside the music world.

Many people wonder how these musicians can keep up. How do they keep going? How is it that they have accomplished so much in just one lifetime? No one, not even the Rolling Stones themselves, can answer that question. But the fact remains that they keep going and going. The Rolling Stones are just as popular today as they ever were, if not more popular. One can only imagine what the band will offer the world next.

TIMELINE

1936—Bill Wyman is born on October 24 in Penge, London.

1941—Charlie Watts is born on June 2 in Neasden, London.

1942—Brian Jones is born on February 28 in Cheltenham, Gloucestershire.

1943—Mick Jagger is born on July 26 in Dartford, Kent; Keith Richards is born on December 18 in Dartford, Kent.

1947—Ronnie Wood is born on June 1 in Hillingdon, Middlesex.

1960—Mick Jagger and Keith Richards meet by chance at a train station. The meeting rekindles their childhood friendship.

1962—The Rolling Stones make their first appearance at the Marquee Club in London; Dick Taylor leaves the band.

1963—Charlie Watts joins the Rolling Stones as their new drummer.

1964—The Rolling Stones first visit the United States.

1965—The Rolling Stones make their first number-one hit in the United States with their single, "Satisfaction."

1967—Mick Jagger and Keith Richards each spend one
night in jail for possessing illegal drugs.

1969—Brian Jones is found dead in his swimming pool
on July 3; on December 6, a concert attendee
is stabbed to death at Altamont Speedway,
San Francisco, California.

1971—The Rolling Stones sign with Atlantic Records.

1975—Ronnie Wood first plays with the Rolling
Stones.

1977—Keith Richards is found guilty of possessing
cocaine.

1979—Keith Richards releases his first solo work.

1984—Mick Jagger sings with Michael Jackson on
single "State of Shock."

1986—The Rolling Stones receive a Lifetime
Achievement Grammy Award.

1989—The Rolling Stones are inducted into the
Rock and Roll Hall of Fame.

1990—Keith Richards suffers a severe finger infection;
Ronnie Wood breaks both of his legs in a car
crash.

1994—The Rolling Stones produce the first concert
over the Internet.

1998—Ronnie Wood's boat explodes while he travels the Brazilian coast; Keith Richards falls off a ladder in his home library and sustains chest and rib injuries.

2001—Mick Jagger focuses on his film company as the movie *Enigma* is released.

2002—The Rolling Stones release their own brand of clothing.

2003—Mick Jagger receives knighthood.

2004—Charlie Watts recovers from throat cancer.

2006—A Bigger Bang Tour is officially named the most moneymaking tour in history. The tour brought in more than $437 million.

2008—The Rolling Stones team up with film director Martin Scorsese and create the documentary concert film *Shine a Light*.

2009—The Rolling Stones are offered millions of dollars to tour the United States.

SELECTED DISCOGRAPHY

1964 *The Rolling Stones (United Kingdom)*

1965 *The Rolling Stones, Now! (United States)*

December's Children (And Everybody's)

1966 *Aftermath*

1967 *Flowers*

Their Satanic Majesties Request

1968 *Beggars Banquet*

1969 *Let It Bleed*

1971 *Sticky Fingers*

1972 *Exile on Main St.*

1973 *Goat's Head Soup*

1975 *Metamorphosis*

1976 *Black and Blue*

1981 *Tattoo You*

1989 *Steel Wheels*

1994 *Voodoo Lounge*

1997 *Bridges to Babylon*

2002 *Forty Licks*

2005 *A Bigger Bang*

2008 *Shine a Light*

CONCERT TOURS

1963 British Tour 1963

1964 First British Tour

First American Tour

1965 Far East Tour

Second British Tour

Second American Tour

1966 Australasian Tour

1967 European Tour

1969 American Tour

1971 U.K. Tour

1976 Tour of Europe

1978 U.S. Tour

1981 American Tour

1989–1990 Steel Wheels Tour

1994–1995 Voodoo Lounge Tour

1997–1998 Bridges to Babylon Tour

1999 No Security Tour

2002–2003 Licks Tour

2005–2007 A Bigger Bang Tour

GLOSSARY

amplifier—A device that, when combined with a loudspeaker, is used to increase the volume of electric instruments such as guitars and keyboards.

authoritative—Originating from an official source and requiring obedience.

blackouts—A period when lights must be covered or turned off to avoid being seen by enemy attackers during a war or battle setting.

British Invasion—A term used to describe the movement of British musicians into the U.S. music industry during the 1960s.

campaign—A series of military attacks focused on a certain area.

chaos—Complete disorder and confusion.

dulcimer—A musical instrument in which strings are stretched across a frame and struck with small hammers.

field hollers—Short verses or songs chanted by slaves working in the fields.

fret charts—Charts on paper that describe where a musician is to place the fingers on a guitar in order to create a certain note or chord.

gig—A slang term used to describe a show or job at which a band is hired to play.

gramophone—An old-fashioned term for a record player.

integrity—The quality of being honest and highly moral.

marimba—A low-toned musical instrument similar to a xylophone that is struck with padded sticks.

mesmerize—To completely consume one's attention as if hypnotized.

oppressive—Placing extreme hardship on a group, especially a minority or person of lesser power.

plantations—Large farms cultivated by laborers who also live on the estate, most often under difficult conditions of poverty.

ration—A standard and fixed amount of a material or supply allowed to a person.

truncheon—A thick, short stick used as a weapon and carried by a police officer.

winklepickers—Short boots or shoes characterized by extremely long and pointed toes. They were most often worn by rock musicians.

CHAPTER NOTES

Chapter 1: Frenzied Fans

1. Bent Rej, *The Rolling Stones in the Beginning* (Buffalo, N.Y.: Firefly Books, 2006), p. 221.
2. Ibid., p. 197.
3. Bill Wyman, *Rolling With the Stones* (New York: DK Publishing, Inc., 2002), p. 202.
4. Rej, p. 204.
5. Ibid., p. 216.
6. Ibid., p. 210.
7. Ibid., p. 222.
8. Wyman, p. 202.
9. Rej, p. 223.
10. Ibid., p. 222.

Chapter 2: The Lives of Legends

1. Christopher Sandford, *Mick Jagger: Rebel Knight* (London, United Kingdom: Omnibus Press, 2003), p. 13.
2. Jann S. Wenner, "Jagger Remembers," *Rolling Stone*, December 14, 1995, <http://www.rollingstone.com/news/coverstory/mick_jagger_remembers> (March 17, 2008), p. 4.
3. Sandford, p. 16.
4. Ibid., p. 18.
5. Ibid.

6. Ibid., p. 15.

7. Christopher Sandford, *Keith Richards: Satisfaction* (New York: Carroll and Graf Publishers, 2003), p. 2.

8. Bill Wyman, *Rolling With the Stones* (New York: DK Publishing, Inc., 2002), p. 21.

9. The Rolling Stones, *According to the Rolling Stones,* ed. Dora Loewenstein and Philip Dodd (San Francisco, Calif.: Chronicle Books, 2003), p. 19.

10. Ibid.

11. Sandford, *Keith Richards: Satisfaction,* p. 17.

12. Ibid., p. 18.

13. The Rolling Stones, p. 14.

14. Sandford, *Keith Richards: Satisfaction,* p. 24.

15. Bent Rej, *The Rolling Stones in the Beginning* (Buffalo, N.Y.: Firefly Books, 2006), p. 263.

16. Wyman, *Rolling With the Stones,* p. 22.

17. Ibid., p. 23.

18. Gloria Shepherd, *Brian Jones Straight From the Heart* (Johnstown, Colo.: High Seas Publishing, 2007), p. 7.

19. Ibid., p. xxvi.

20. Ibid., p. 13.

21. Ibid., p. 9.

22. Ibid., p. 10.

23. Ibid., p. xxv.

24. Bill Wyman, *Stone Alone: The Story of a Rock 'n' Roll Band* (New York: Da Capo Press, 1997), p. 34.

25. Ibid.

26. Ibid., p. 49.

27. Rej., p. 163.

28. Wyman, *Stone Alone*, p. 55.

29. Rej, p. 226.

30. Alan Clayson, *Charlie Watts* (London, United Kingdom: Sanctuary Publishing Limited, 2004), p. 14.

31. Ibid., p. 15.

32. Ibid., p. 16.

33. Rej, p. 226.

34. Ronnie Wood, *Ronnie Wood: The Autobiography* (New York: St. Martin's Press, 2007), p. 3.

35. Ibid., p. 6.

36. Ibid., p. 8.

37. Ibid., p. 7.

38. Ibid., p. 20.

39. Ibid.

40. Ibid., p. 24.

41. Ibid., p. 26.

Chapter 3: Boys With the Blues

1. Jann S. Wenner, "Jagger Remembers," *Rolling Stone,* December 14, 1995, <http://www.rollingstone.com/news/coverstory/mick_jagger_remembers> (March 17, 2008), p. 5.

2. Ibid.

3. Christopher Sandford, *Keith Richards:*

Satisfaction (New York: Carroll and Graf Publishers, 2004), p. 34.

4. Wenner, p. 6.

5. Sandford, p. 36.

6. "The Rolling Stones," *Rock and Roll Hall of Fame and Museum*, n.d., <http://www.rockhall.com/inductee/the-rolling-stones> (May 19, 2008).

7. Ibid.

8. Ibid., p. 2.

9. Sandford, p. 43.

10. Ibid.

11. Gloria Shepherd, *Brian Jones Straight From the Heart* (Johnstown, Colo.: High Seas Publishing, 2007), p. 61.

12. Bill Wyman, *Stone Alone: The Story of a Rock 'n' Roll Band* (New York: De Capo Press, 1997), p. 152.

13. Ibid., p. 151.

14. Shepherd, p. 64.

15. Wyman, p. 213.

16. Shepherd, p. 139.

17. "The Rolling Stones."

Chapter 4: Hard Times Hit the United States

1. *Encyclopedia Britannica,* s.v. "John F. Kennedy," DVD-ROM, Ultimate Reference Suite, Encyclopedia Britannica, 2008.

2. *Encarta Encyclopedia,* s.v. "Communism,"

<http://encarta.msn.com/encyclopedia_
761572241/communism.html> (October 20, 2008).

3. "Vietnam War," *Vietnam War.com,* <http://www.
vietnamwar.com/> (October 20, 2008).

4. Todd Leopold, "When the Beatles Hit America,"
CNN Entertainment, February 10, 2004, <http://
edition.cnn.com/2004/SHOWBIZ/Music/02/05/
beatles.40/> (October 20, 2008).

5. Ibid.

6. "The Beatles," *Rock and Roll Hall of Fame and
Museum,* n.d., <http://www.rockhall.com/
inductee/the-beatles> (October 20, 2008).

7. Jonathan Lamy, "The American Recording
Industry Announces Its Artists of the Century,"
RIAA News Room, November 10, 1999, <http://
www.riaa.com/newsitem.php?news_year_filter=
1999&resultpage=2&id=3ABF3EC8-EF5B-58F9-
E949-3B57F5E313DF> (October 20, 2008).

8. *Encyclopedia Britannica,* s.v. "British Invasion:
The Kinks," (by Jon Savage) <http://search.
eb.com/britishinvasion/Kinksindex.html>
(October 20, 2008).

9. "The Story of the Who," *The Who Official Band
Website,* n.d., <http://www.thewho.com/index.
php?module=history> (October 20, 2008).

10. "A Short Blues History," *History of Rock,* n.d.,
<http://www.history-of-rock.com/blues.htm>
(October 20, 2008).

11. Ibid.

12. Muddy Waters, *Hard Again*, CD (1977; New York: Sony Music Entertainment, Inc., 2004).

Chapter 5: The Later Years

1. Gloria Shepherd, *Brian Jones Straight From the Heart* (Johnstown, Colo.: High Seas Publishing, 2007), p. 282.

2. Ibid.

3. Ibid., p. 283.

4. "The Rolling Stones," *Rock and Roll Hall of Fame and Museum*, n.d., <http://www.rockhall.com/inductee/the-rolling-stones> (October 20, 2008).

5. Shepherd, p. 299.

6. Ronnie Wood, *Ronnie Wood: The Autobiography* (New York: St. Martin's Press, 2007), p. 94.

7. Jann S. Wenner, "Jagger Remembers," *Rolling Stone,* December 14, 1995, <http://www.rollingstone.com/news/coverstory/mick_jagger_remembers> (March 17, 2008).

8. Christopher Sandford, *Mick Jagger: Rebel Knight* (London, United Kingdom: Omnibus Press, 2003), p. 176.

9. Ibid.

10. Ibid., p. 177.

11. John Burks, "Rock & Roll's Worst Day," *Rolling Stone,* February 7, 1970, <http://rollingstone.com/

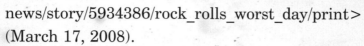

news/story/5934386/rock_rolls_worst_day/print>
(March 17, 2008).

12. Wenner, p. 3.

13. Wood, p. 109.

14. Ibid., p. 110.

15. Ibid.

16. Ibid.

17. Ibid., p. 111.

18. "The Rolling Stones."

Chapter 6: Where Are They Now?

1. "Concert for New York City Over $30 Million Raised," *VH1.com*, n.d., <http://www.vh1.com/news/features/america_united?> (October 14, 2008).

2. "Concert for New York City, October 20, 2001" (live performance).

3. "It's Only Rock 'n Roll," *The Rolling Stones Fan Club*, n.d., <http://www.iorr.org/> (October 14, 2008).

4. "The SARS Report: What Is Really Happening In Toronto?" *MedSci Communications*, April 7, 2003, <http://www.medscicommunications.com/toronto-sars-report.htm> (October 14, 2008).

5. "AC/DC Molson Canadian Rocks Downsview Park," *Crabsody in Blue*, July 30, 2003, <http://www.crabsodyinblue.com/acdctoronto2003.htm> (October 21, 2008).

6. "Bombardier Welcomes the 'Molson Canadian Rocks for Toronto Featuring Rolling Stones' Concert to Its Toronto Site," *Business Services Industry: Gale Cengage Learning,* July 28, 2003, <http://findarticles.com/p/articles/mi_m0EIN/ is_2003_July_28/ai_105955521> (October 14, 2008).

7. "Rolling Stones Headline Concert," *CBC Archives,* n.d., <http://archives.cbc.ca/arts_entertainment/ music/clips/8601/> (October 21, 2008).

8. "Keith Richards 'Tree Fall' Injury," *BBC News,* April 29, 2006, <http://news.bbc.co.uk/2/hi/ entertainment/4957948.stm> (October 14, 2008).

9. "Ronnie Wood Checks Into Rehab," *Female First*, June 14, 2006, <http://www.femalefirst.co.uk/ celebrity/Ronnie+Wood-10215.html> (October 14, 2008).

10. *Shine a Light*, DVD, directed by Martin Scorsese (Los Angeles, Calif.: Paramount Classics, 2008).

11. "*Shine a Light* Recent Reviews," *Flixster,* August 31, 2008, <http://www.flixster.com/movie/ shine-a-light> (October 14, 2008).

12. David Wild, "Johnny Depp and Keith Richards: *Pirates of the Caribbean's* Blood Brothers," *Rolling Stone*, May 31, 2007, <http://rollingstone. com/news/story/14474260/ johnny_depp_keith_ richards_pirates_of_the_caribbeans_blood_ brothers/print> (October 21, 2008).

13. "Keith Richards' Guitar Museum," *Female First*, April 21, 2008, <http://www.femalefirst.co.uk/celebrity/Keith+Richards-20612.html> (October 21, 2008).

14. Ibid.

15. Tim Spanton, "Interview With Keith Richards," *The Sun: Celeb Interviews*, March 31, 2008, <http://www.thesun.co.uk.sol.homepage/showbiz/bizarre/celeb_interviews/article 978486.ece> (October 14, 2008).

16. "Synopsis," *Enigma—The Movie*, <http://www.thefilmfactory.co.uk/enigma/main.html> (April 30, 2009).

17. "About the Film," *The Women*, <http://thewomen.warnerbros.com/index.html> (October 14, 2008).

18. "Jagger Knighthood: Richards Rages," *CNN.com*, December 4, 2003, <http://www.cnn.com/2003/SHOWBIZ/Music/12/04/jagger.richards.reut/> (October 14, 2008).

19. "Stones Row Over Jagger Knighthood," *BBC News*, December 4, 2003, <http://news.bbc.co.uk/2/hi/entertainment/3290411.stm> (October 14, 2008).

20. Michael Askounes, "Charlie Watts Jim Keltner Project," *All About Jazz*, n.d., <http://www.allaboutjazz.com/php/article.php?id=6137> (October 14, 2008).

21. Alan Clayson, *Charlie Watts* (London, United

Kingdom: Sanctuary Publishing Limited, 2004),
p. 156.

22. Nick Constable, "Wife of Rolling Stone Charlie
Watts Locked in Legal Row After Snatching Back
Horse from Rivals," *Mail Online*, August 24,
2008, <http://www.dailymail.co.uk/news/article-
1048669/Wife-Rolling-Stone-Charlie-Watts-locked-
legal-row-snatching-4-000-horse-rivals.html>
(October 14, 2008).

23. Valentine Low, "Ronnie's Ivy League," *This Is
London: The Evening Standard*, n.d., <http://
www.limelightagency.com/Ronnie-Wood/Press/
londons-ivy.html> (October 14, 2008).

24. Ronnie Wood, *Ronnie Wood: The Autobiography*
(New York: St. Martin's Press, 2007), p. 317.

25. Ibid.

26. "Ron Wood's Paintings Too Expensive for Mick
Jagger," *Starpulse Entertainment News Blog*,
February 8, 2008, <http://www.starpulse.com/news/
index.php/2008/02/08/ ron_wood_s_paintings_too_
expensive_for_m> (October 14, 2008).

FURTHER READING

Books

Riggs, Kate. *Rock 'n' Roll Music*. Mankato, Minn.: Creative Education, 2008.

Rosen, Steven. *History of Rock*. New York: Crabtree Publishing Company, 2009.

Schaefer, A.R. *Forming a Band*. Mankato, Minn.: Capstone High-Interest Books, 2004.

Schlesinger, Ethan. *The Rolling Stones*. Broomall, Pa.: Mason Crest Publishers, 2007.

Tanner, Mike. *Flat-out Rock: Ten Great Bands of the '60s*. Toronto: Annick Press, 2006.

Wyman, Bill, with Richard Havers. *Rolling with the Stones*. New York: DK Pub., 2002.

Internet Addresses

Rolling Stones
<http://www.rollingstones.com/archive/>

Rock and Roll Hall of Fame + Museum: The Rolling Stones
<http://www.rockhall.com/inductee/the-rolling-stones>

INDEX